POETRY

March 2013

FOUNDED IN 1912 BY HARRIET MONROE

VOLUME CCI ꞏ NUMBER 6

CONTENTS

March 2013

POEMS

REMEMBERING POETS

A FEW MORE DON'TS

COMMENT

Editor	CHRISTIAN WIMAN
Senior Editor	DON SHARE
Associate Editor	FRED SASAKI
Managing Editor	VALERIE JEAN JOHNSON
Editorial Assistant	LINDSAY GARBUTT
Consulting Editor	CHRISTINA PUGH
Art Direction	WINTERHOUSE STUDIO

COVER ART BY DIANA SUDYKA
"It Was Often Seen Wandering," 2012

POETRYMAGAZINE.ORG

A PUBLICATION OF THE

POETRY FOUNDATION

PRINTED BY CADMUS PROFESSIONAL COMMUNICATIONS, US

Poetry · March 2013 · Volume 201 · Number 6

Poetry (ISSN: 0032-2032) is published monthly, except bimonthly July/August, by the Poetry Foundation. Address editorial correspondence to 61 W. Superior St., Chicago, IL 60654. Individual subscription rates: $35.00 per year domestic; $47.00 per year foreign. Library/institutional subscription rates: $38.00 per year domestic; $50.00 per year foreign. Single copies $3.75, plus $1.75 postage, for current issue; $4.25, plus $1.75 postage, for back issues. Address new subscriptions, renewals, and related correspondence to Poetry, PO 421141, Palm Coast, FL 32142-1141 or call 800.327.6976. Periodicals postage paid at Chicago, IL, and additional mailing offices. POSTMASTER: Send address changes to Poetry, PO Box 421141, Palm Coast, FL 32142-1141. All rights reserved. Copyright © 2013 by the Poetry Foundation. Double issues cover two months but bear only one number. Volumes that include double issues comprise numbers 1 through 5. Indexed in "Access," "Humanities International Complete," "Book Review Index," "The Index of American Periodical Verse," "Poem Finder," and "Popular Periodical Index." Manuscripts cannot be returned and will be destroyed unless accompanied by a stamped, self-addressed envelope, or by international reply coupons and a self-addressed envelope from writers living abroad. Copying done for other than personal or internal reference use without the expressed permission of the Poetry Foundation is prohibited. Requests for special permission or bulk orders should be addressed to the Poetry Foundation. Available in braille from the National Library Service for the Blind and Physically Handicapped. Available on microfilm and microfiche through National Archive Publishing Company, Ann Arbor, MI. Digital archive available at JSTOR.org. Distributed to bookstores by Ingram Periodicals, Source Interlink, Ubiquity Distributors, and Central Books in the UK.

POEMS

MICHAEL HOFMANN

Venice Beach

Annihilating all that's made
To a green thought in a green shade.
— Andrew Marvell

These are all thoughts — of course. At the edge of the ocean with
    nowhere to go,
the nearest land three thousand miles away and under different
    management,

the diving sun another thirty thousand times that, there is no reality,
only these parlous notions, messages, statements, stylings on the
    edge of extinction.

Little petillas. A kind of spontaneous zoo of human recency and
    arrival
and promontory variorum. Imprudent comb-over thoughts,

rigid and proud eye-catching false thoughts, little jiggling thoughts,
intricate braided-beard thoughts the product of much misplaced
    patience,

product placement thoughts (which are rather elementary,
and are almost a contradiction in terms), unlike myriad highly-
    evolved

dog thoughts (no mutts here), pushing a baby in a three-wheeled
    stroller
whilst running very hard in no shirt and six-pack thoughts,

this a development on the now-obsolete egg and paddle
(what it does to the infant to be impelled at such a rate into the future

whilst facing backwards like an Aeroflot passenger is not recorded —
not that forward is necessarily better), high-concept silky-swishing
    Afghan hound thoughts,

intrusive bum thoughts, hapless and homeless panhandler thoughts
(a *smarte carte* loaded with undesirables never far to seek),

low-slung belly-dragging beagle thoughts little better
than the serpent in the Bible, holding hands Adam and Eve thoughts,

foot-shuffling Zimmer frame thoughts, "revolution in mobility"
    wheelchair and gravel thoughts,
pushed by most likely an illegal attendant borderline thoughts,

candy-striped T-shirt and shorts thoughts, cut-off thoughts,
paired with sometimes nothing more than a bikini top, those three-
    quarter length

thin and probably amphibious trousers, worn without socks, that
    men go in for,
suggestive of adaptability and resourcefulness thoughts,

standard over-loud mobile thoughts, ("our relationship is ... "),
lying immobile on the grass on your back mobile thoughts

(these are different), tourist thoughts, an unexpected preponderance
    of Russian thoughts
(though with residential qualifications), borscht belt leopard skin
    thoughts

dripping with gold and eccentric lamentations, dog and baby both
    thoughts
(these last thought to be ideally-balanced), high-stepping poodle
    thoughts

like a four-wheel drive with little intelligence in rough country,
furiously texting in the glare with all thumbs to the pump thoughts,

being at least half elsewhere, baseball cap thoughts rife with deter-
    mination,
slightly dated straw hat thoughts, reverse baseball cap also thoughts.

LV

The luncheon voucher years
(the bus pass and digitized medical record
always in the inside pocket come later,
and the constant orientation to the nearest hospital).
The years of "sir" (long past "mate," much less "dearie"),
of invisibility, of woozy pacifism,
of the preemptive smile of the hard-of-hearing,

of stiff joints and the small pains
that will do me in. The ninth complement
of fresh — stale — cells, the Late Middle Years
(say, 1400 AD — on the geological calendar),
the years of the incalculable spreading middle,
the years of speculatively counting down
from an unknown terminus,

because the whole long stack —
shale, vertebrae, pancakes, platelets, plates —
won't balance anymore, and doesn't correspond anyway
to the thing behind the eyes that says "I"
and feels uncertain green and treble
and wants its kilt as it climbs up to the lectern to blush
and read "thou didst not abhor the virgin's womb."

The years of taking the stairs two at a time
(though not at weekends)
a bizarre debt to Dino Buzzati's *Tartar Steppe*,
the years of a deliberate lightness of tread,
perceived as a nod to Franz Josef
thinking with his knees and rubber-tired Viennese *Fiaker*.
The years when the dead are starting to stack up.

The years of incuriosity and *novarum rerum*
in*cupidissimus*, the years of cheap acquisition
and irresponsible postponement, or cheap
postponement and irresponsible acquisition,
of listlessness, of miniaturism, of irascibility,
of being soft on myself, of being hard on myself,
and neither knowing nor especially caring which.

The years of re-reading (at arm's length).
The fiercely objected-to professional years,
the appalling indulgent years, the years of no challenge
and comfort zone and safely within my borders.
The years of no impressions and little memory.

The years of standing in elevators
under the elevator lights in the elevator mirror,
feeling and looking like leathered frizz,
an old cheese-topped dish under an infrared hot plate.

The years of one over the thirst
and another one over the hunger, of insomnia
and sleeping in, of creases and pouches and heaviness
and the hairdresser offering to trim my eyebrows.
The years of the unbeautiful corpse in preparation.
The years to choose: *sild*, or *flamber*
...?

DOUGLAS KEARNEY

The Labor of Stagger Lee: Boar

pigs prey to piggishnesses. get ate from the rooter to the tooter.
I'm a hog for you baby, I can't get enough go the wolfish crooner.
the gust buffeted porker roll in the hay or laid down
    in twig rapine. let me in, let me in.

    no drum-gut, Stagger's stomach a tenement:
his deadeye bigger than his brick house.
Stagger Lee live by the want and die by the noose,
whose greedy void like a whorehouse
    full of empties getting full. can't get enough!
rumored Stagger would root through pussy
to plumb a fat boy. here piggy! what Lee see he seize.
manful, ham-fisted. sorry Billy,
    your name *mud* and who love dirt like swine?
they get in it like a straw house. it'll be cold out
before Lee admit his squeals weren't howls.
he got down. he get dirty.

Dolphins at Seven Weeks

Inward lush unpetaling purpose in pink blooms of sleep, and I no longer needed to be separate. I was living there then, at the edge of the sea. And my friends came to visit, trying for a baby, not sure how to read me on that island of dozy sunlight. And there it was: familiarity edged with fear, the way we'd feed each other sandwiches and wonder if we should have wanted something other. We walked the folded cliffs over conifer fronds and mud runneling rocks slick with dropped fruit and rotting camellias to pause at the first ridge. We looked through high pines at the blue moving tides, then his finger caught a snag in the water and another and we saw — glinting fins wheeling the sheen, thousands playing in pods coming closer like the souls slippering into our bodies, attaching to matter as flippers angle into a ferrying strand. We too are a species, I realized. We too could know that as joy.

Kauai

We've come back to the site of her
conception. She calls it *why*

and cries all night,
sleepless, wild.

It seems the way is always
floating and the goal —

to live so the ghosts we were
don't trail us and echo.

I think we are inside a flower,
under a pollen of stars vast as scattered sand.

The air pulses with perfume,
flowers calling to flowers and the ferrying air.

But my eyes are thin and elsewhere.
I am thinking, maybe

even coming into the soul
is a difficult birth, squeezed by the body's vise.

My bent legs like pincers
or the vegetable petals of some tropical flower.

Even my mind gripped by the folds
of the flesh, how the cells keep twinning

themselves out toward complexity.
The tulip trees of the valley

spread their bone canopies into slick green leaves
and fire flowers deep as cups.

Their cups fill with rain, rain
drinks the leaves drinking rain.

I can't begin to explain.
How on this porous peak of stone in the sea

our daughter came into me.
Little flick of a fish I could not see.

I was just learning to be human
and upright among all that life.

And what was real was stranger
than night with its dust of unnamed suns.

It was the beyond in us. And she was.

DAN BROWN

Girl-Watching

In the years I've been at this
(Lots, not to be precise)
You'd think that once or twice
At least I would have seen
Some anomalies. I mean
Some major ones. As in
Not feet but little wheels,
Or crests like cockatiels'.
Where are they keeping the girls
With a chrome exterior,
Or an extra derriere?
Apparently nowhere.
Assuming my sample's valid,
The pool is limited
To the standard types I've tallied;
Such variance as there is
In the usual congeries
Of physiognomies —
And yet enough of it
To be worth the looking at.
The walking by, for that,
Of the same girl over and over
Would be no cross to bear
If it were that one there.

Judo

I.e., the kind of verse
That doesn't try to force
People to their knees
(Seeing as it sees
To people's being thrown
By forces of their own).

Why I Never Applied Myself to Pool

Not that I lacked an eye entirely,
But give me an oblique enough kiss
To visualize, and my eye said "See ya later."
A little practice might have sharpened it,
But what was needed here was not as much
A sharper as a higher order eye,
A whole other orb altogether.

Nose Job

An unexpected consequence
Of mine (and one that shows how well
It really went, in a scary sense)
Is at its most perceptible
When I happen to observe a nose
With the hump of which my nose is rid
(Though not my psyche, you'd suppose)
And feel the sighting visited
By what a lord might call a kind
Of pity: distant, tinged with scorn ...
A thing you'd more expect to find
In someone to his beauty born.

ANTHONY OPAL

Sonnet

you have lipstick on your collar I say
to my father the priest that's just the Blood
of Christ my son he replies by and by
(the milky thigh of Mary in my mind)
William Blake's eyes aligning in the snow
a statue outside London simply called
"The Heretic" where birds sit and shit and
live out their days in unconscious praise
of that third space between language and the
mute object as sunlight pours through
the stained glass at the Lincoln Park Zoo
where I saw the lions pacing and you
told me to always remember that the cage
is for the protection of the captor

AMY GERSTLER

Bon Courage

Why are the woods so alluring? A forest appears
to a young girl one morning as she combs
the dreams out of her hair. The trees rustle
and whisper, shimmer and hiss. The forest
opens and closes, a door loose on its hinges,
banging in a strong wind. Everything in the dim
kitchen: the basin, the jug, the skillet, the churn,
snickers scornfully. In this way a maiden
is driven toward the dangers of a forest,
but the forest is our subject, not this young girl.

She's glad to lie down with trees towering all around.
A certain euphoria sets in. She feels molecular,
bedeviled, senses someone gently pulling her hair,
tingles with kisses she won't receive for years.
Three felled trees, a sort of chorus, narrate
her thoughts, or rather channel theirs through her,
or rather subject her to their peculiar verbal
restlessness ... *our deepening need for non-being* intones
the largest and most decayed tree, mid-sentence.
I'm not one of you squeaks the shattered sapling,

blackened by lightning. Their words become metallic
spangles shivering the air. *Will I forget the way home?*
the third blurts. *Why do I feel like I'm hiding in a giant's nostril?*
the oldest prone pine wants to know. *Are we being freed
from matter?* the sapling asks. *Insects are well-intentioned,*
offers the third tree, by way of consolation. *Will it grow
impossible to think a thought through to its end?* gasps the sapling,
adding in a panicky voice, *I'm becoming spongy!* The girl
feels her hands attach to some distant body. She rises
to leave, relieved these trees are not talking about her.

Hoffnung

He fancies his chances are good with her,
unaware that in the years since the war

she has come to prefer women whose cunts
taste like mustard. To pin one's hopes on

a bark-colored moth, its wings crinkled
like crepe paper, a moth affixed high

on the kitchen wall, frozen for days where
it will likely die in noble clinging mode

just under the cobwebby heating vent,
is to confirm your need for more friends

and a greater daily quota of sunlight.
To raise C.'s hopes that T. can stop

drinking and then to liken those
hopes to fields of undulating grain,

alfalfa perhaps, is to wish C. hip deep
in acres of unscythed denial. The blind

typist hopes she'll be hired tonight without
her disability becoming an issue. L. said he felt

hope's rhizomes race throughout his body,
radiating in all directions, like some incipient

disease he'd been fighting since childhood.
Hope, he said, it's as insidious as bitterness.

If mother earth only knew how much we
loved one another she would creak, shudder,

and split like a macheted melon, releasing
the fiery ball of molten hope at her core.

Sea Foam Palace

(Bubbling and spuming
as if trying to talk under
water, I address you thus:)
Must I pretend not to love
you (in your present bloom,
your present perfection — soul
encased in fleshly relevance)
so you won't believe me
just another seabed denizen
vying for your blessed attention?
Some of us (but not you)
are so loosely moored
to our bodies we can
barely walk a straight line,
remaining (most days) only
marginally conscious.
We stagger and shudder
as buckets of blood or sperm
or chocolate mousse or spittle
or lymph or sludge sluice
continually through us ...

I love the way you wear your
face, how you ride this life.
I delight in the sight of you,
your nervous, inquisitive eyes,
though I try to act otherwise.
Being stoned out of thy mind
only amps up thy fearsome
brain wattage. Pardon my
frontal offensive, dear chum.
Forgive my word-churn, my
drift, the ways this text message
has gotten all frothy. How was it
you became holy to me? Should

I resist, furiously? Is this your
true visage, shaken free, flashing
glimpses of what underlies
the world we can see? *Do not forget me*
murmurs something nibbled
by fish under the sea.

After dark you're quick-silvery,
wet/slick/glistening. Don't
make me chase you, dragging
my heavy caresses, a pair of
awkward, serrated claws,
hither and yon. Give me a swig
of whatever you're drinking,
to put me in tune with the cosmos's
relentless melt, with the rhythms
of dish-washing, corn-shucking,
hard-fucking, bed-wetting, and
the folding of bones of other loves
into well-dug graves … may we
never become lost to the world.

AMIT MAJMUDAR

Save the Candor

Every tripod-
toting birder
knows it never
nests on urban

girders. Even
fences set its
scalded-crimson
head askew, its

waddle swinging,
wings akimbo.
Few have got it
on their lists and

fewer still have
caught it singing,
this endangered
North American

candor, cousin
of the done-in
dodo, big-eyed
Big Sur tremor-

tenor — only
ten or twenty
hang glide over
Modoc County,

humbly numbered
(as their days are)
for us crazy
crown- and throat- and

belly-gazers.
Any niche as
fragile as a
candor's renders

its extinction
certain. We can
sabotage its
habitat with

half a laugh or
quarter murmur,
fluster coveys
worth of candors

off their branches,
which, abandoned,
soon are little
more than snarking-

grounds for minor
birds, the common
snipe, the yellow-
bellied bittern.

JOANNE DOMINIQUE DWYER

Beaded Baby Moccasins

If love is like a doll's shoe —
the color of nascent snow
that laces over the ankle
or the polychromatic beaded baby moccasins
we saw lying in the museum drawer
that belonged to an infant from a sea tribe of seal hunters.
Or the rutilant pink blossoms
of the locust tree that bloomed in the dark
while I slept dreaming of my arrival
on a red-eye wearing a long to the floor skirt —
not of a postulant, but of a flower vendor
or a woman covering disfigurement.
Freud believed that religious faith
is a wish-fulfilling illusion.
I can't locate faith in a carved or uncarved pew.
I'm more focused on the altar boy's shoes.
Under his white robe he's wearing a man's black loafers
vastly oversized for his small feet with
sufficient spare space for a coyote den in each toe.
I want to buy him a kite.
If love is a mezzanine floor we will not fall from,
a hand holding back my hair from my face
as I'm sick on the side of the bus.
The mouth so at home in the vicinity of pavement.
Pew also means to enclose, as in men who were
as willingly pewed in the parish church
as their sheep were in night folds.
Freud also believed civilized life imposes suffering,
yet he always wore a dinner jacket.
We delaminate layers of old paint
bleach sheets in the shade.
I take out the oily ham from the beans,
the unflattering photos from the folio,
the quotes about repressed homosexuality
being the reason Sigmund's patient Little Hans
is afraid of horses.

DAVID BARBER

Aria

What if it were possible to vanquish
All this shame with a wash of varnish
Instead of wishing the stain would vanish?

What if you gave it a glossy finish?
What if there were a way to burnish
All this foolishness, all the anguish?

What if you gave yourself leave to ravish
All these ravages with famished relish?
What if this were your way to flourish?

What if the self you love to punish —
Knavish, peevish, wolfish, sheepish —
Were all slicked up in something lavish?

Why so squeamish? Why make a fetish
Out of everything you must relinquish?
Why not embellish what you can't abolish?

What would be left if you couldn't brandish
All the slavishness you've failed to banish?
What would you be without this gibberish?

What if the true worth of the varnish
Were to replenish your resolve to vanquish
Every vain wish before you vanish?

Corn Maze

Here is where
You can get nowhere
Faster than ever
As you go under
Deeper and deeper

In the fertile smother
Of another acre
Like any other
You can't peer over
And then another

And everywhere
You veer or hare
There you are
Farther and farther
Afield than before

But on you blunder
In the verdant meander
As if the answer
To looking for cover
Were to bewilder

Your inner minotaur
And near and far were
Neither here nor there
And where you are
Is where you were

Lacrimarium

Were there a tear
To spare, where better
To be sure the gesture
Would linger than here
In its own little bottle
Blown from a hot bubble
To mirror a tear.

And were there more
Than one could bear,
So much the better
In the hereafter for
The begetter, a little
Vessel to stopper
Sorrow beyond measure.

And were there a tear
Too few, far better to hire
A weeper, for where
But in a tearful little
Jigger does it figure
No one need settle for
Less than a fair share.

BRUCE SNIDER

Devotions

1

Nothing passes, Lord, but what you allow.
Mornings the milky sap on my knuckles
burns. Last night the piglets fought then suckled
in the barn. Still no word. Our one cow
grazes but won't come in. The pamphlets say:
Patience is required. I say, let's try again
but John blames the state, the neighbors, the way
we wrote our bios, filling out the forms.
Across the road our neighbor starts his truck
while God, feather by feather, downs a wren —
swollen, its black eyes shiny, small dark tongue.
In the drainpipe, something slithers wet and stuck.
A race runner? A ground skink shedding skin?
Lizards, John tells me, *can't bear live young.*

2

John tells me: *lizards can't bear live young.*
Another of God's mysteries: hard rain
muddying the corn. The kind woman
at the agency said, *it takes longer for certain*
types of couples. Trash smoke rises like prayer,
the neighbor burning insulation from his shed.
He shows his son how to bind fence where
a crippled chicken pecks at scattered feed.
They talk, lean close. Rusted toys fill
the side yard: old trucks, a bicycle tire,
a punctured red bucket now a sieve.
In the back acre, ram mounts ewe, the whole
field coupling late spring. When John walks by,
I kiss him. Most days we keep to ourselves.

3

I kiss him most days. We keep to ourselves
by the roadside. Two greasy boxes; a sign:
FREE. We take the runt, her warm body beside
us in the truck, milk-breathed and unwormed.
I imagine her shuddering out of the womb, wet
ground covered with slime. Strange to think
of her moving inside some animal's gut,
the source of each day's warm alien kick.
At home John makes her a bed from old
field shirts, a soap and vinegar bath for fleas
while in my lap she chews my hand and shivers.
I brush her fuzzy scruff, the too-large head.
She nips at my finger that holds a piece of cheese,
her wet tongue asking what a man can mother.

4

Even I doubt how a man can mother
when I see the neighbor shout, chuck a stone
at his son. When I shoot him a look, he turns:
mind your own business. The hot sun withers
the peonies John planted on the side of the hill,
dirt gone hard with the sudden change of weather.
Sweating, I mow the lawn, pick up shell
casings in the yard, the crow's strict feathers.
All day I want to break something, stick
a fork in the fan blades to feel the pinch.
Coming home late again from the shop,
John carries two rabbits slung from a hook.
He cleans, for hours, his rifle on the porch.
Above us: the moon rises. An easy shot.

5

Above us the sun rises, bright and hot,
steaming the back pond where black flies stall.
In the pasture, our neighbor castrates his bulls
using a spreading tool with red rubber slats.
The restless cattle graze an unshorn meadow.
On TV: a baby in Toledo in a locked car.
The mother went to work and forgot, windows
up in summer's heat. The camera blurs
over the lot as a medic lifts the blanketed heap
from the back seat in the crew's full view.
Gawkers circle. The mother weeps. Watching,
I can peaches, letting the pale fruit darken.
Beyond the window, bulls still graze the field.
They feed. The bloodless sacks swing, blacken.

6

Steer feed. The bloodless sacks hang, blackened.
On the radio: Haggard's *I'd rather be gone*.
John tends to ordinary things: replaces the drainpipe in the kitchen sink, sharpens knives again.
I watch the neighbor teach his son to paint
the tool shed all afternoon. Soon, they wrestle,
throw a ball, the boy laughing into his father's chest.
In the paper I read the births and deaths,
hear a sudden hammering from behind,
John cursing the warped floorboards, pushing hard
the back door, which still won't budge an inch.
Again today no miracles at hand,
just, in the field, wrens who stab at milkweed pods,
a nuthatch bargaining from its split branch.

7

A nuthatch bargains from its split branch.
Our neighbor stops by, complains our fence
breaks his field. It must be moved eight inches.
The puppy — *Annie*, we call her — pushes
her nose in everything, the front yard, the garden,
finds, across the road, the neighbor's trash —
drags stripped wire, eggshells that harden
like the bones she buries off his porch.
I want to say we are consoled by her,
but each day John jumps when he hears the phone.
We walk over and over down the worn
path to the empty mailbox: *Maybe soon.*
Some nights we make love. We sleep arm to arm.
We wake to our neighbor yelling at his son.

8

Again we wake, our neighbor yelling at his son,
poor kid standing by the porch. Tracking mud,
he backs from the shouting, his father's raised fist.
Later I will see him sulking near our feed shed,
knotting an old piece of garden hose, kicking dust.
I'll smile, ask if he's OK. But right now
I listen to John's quiet breathing beside me.
Faith, they say, is Abraham asked to slaughter
his boy on a mountaintop. But sometimes
it's just the peeling shed in gray weather,
the leather harness softened, then gone rough.
All day today the back pond will teem with carp.
The clover will brighten. For now we lie together
into late morning. Some days, it is enough.

Loop

Curled up in bed,
I'm young
in the old way.

•

One
continuous stroke

without lifting
the pen

as if

"stem, tendril,
stem tendril"

were the words
of a commandment.

•

My next
elliptical loops

read "Praise."

Word

deciphered

at a snail's
pace.

Will

In English
we place a noun
meaning fixed purpose
before our verbs
to create the future
tense.

Here, in the private life
my team invents,
I'm in a floodlit kitchen
like the set
of an old-time ad
for Tide

and I am chopping
something.

Isn't this the past
perfect?
Should I feel nostalgic?

This corn is highly
leveraged

and I'm wearing
a pink slip.

The Eye

These brown piles
of stubble

hills

have failed.

They should be more

·

It should be difficult
but not impossible

to transmute
latitude

into a thought

a god could
hold.

·

Barred light:

dunes coming on
and on.

·

The eye, yes,
must move

to prevent
blank spots

from making themselves
known.

DANIEL HALPERN

Pandemania

There are fewer introductions
In plague years,
Hands held back, jocularity
No longer bellicose,
Even among men.
Breathing's generally wary,
Labored, as they say, when
The end is at hand.
But this is the everyday intake
Of the imperceptible life force,
Willed now, slow —
Well, just cautious
In inhabited air.
As for ongoing dialogue,
No longer an exuberant plosive
To make a point,
But a new squirreling of air space,
A new sense of boundary.
Genghis Khan said the hand
Is the first thing one man gives
To another. Not in this war.
A gesture of limited distance
Now suffices, a nod,
A minor smile or a hand
Slightly raised,
Not in search of its counterpart,
Just a warning within
The acknowledgment to stand back.
Each beautiful stranger a barbarian
Breathing on the other side of the gate.

REMEMBERING POETS

MARK LEVINE

Philip Levine

It is unlikely I would have gone on to live my life in poetry, for better and worse, had I not taken a class with Philip Levine in 1985. I was nineteen at the time. I had never met a published writer, or an artist of any kind, and although I had read a small amount of poetry that had moved me deeply — *The Waste Land*, *Howl*, a few poems of Wallace Stevens, Sylvia Plath, Dylan Thomas — and had even, for some time, carried around a notebook of my own clumsy effusions, somehow it didn't occur to me that "poets" still existed, let alone that someone like me could aspire to be one.

I showed up at his class because his last name was the same as mine. It was the first day of the winter semester of my sophomore year, a Wednesday in January, three days after Ronald Reagan's second inaugural. I went to breakfast in the dark, empty dining hall and came across an article in a student newspaper about a visiting writer named Levine. I had gone to school with other kids named Levine, but their parents were dentists or accountants. My own Levines were a junior high phys ed teacher and a civil servant. According to the article, this Levine was a well-regarded poet. There was a picture of him: gap-toothed, with wavy, unkempt hair, a working man's mustache, and a nose that suggested a turbulent background. The class met at 1:00 PM in the chemistry building, which was on my way across campus. I had no hope of being allowed in — it was reserved, I imagined, for a small group of sophisticates — but I decided to stop by. A year earlier, I had shown up at a similar class to get a glimpse of Susan Sontag, and was quickly turned away.

The room was less crowded than I had expected. Levine wore tennis shoes and an old raincoat. I recall he joked about a student's ridiculous handbag, which was clear vinyl inset with colorful plastic fish. The student seemed put off by the remark, and Levine happily referred to himself as a schmuck. He told us he was glad to have taken the job for the semester because he only had to show up on campus once a week and the salary was excellent. "I demanded what they had to pay me and they said, 'Levine, we can't pay you that much — you've only got a master's, everyone else has a doctorate and they make less.' And I told them, 'That's why I need to be paid more — you don't want to make me feel inferior because of my poor education.'"

He asked our names. I told him mine and he said, "That sounds familiar. I have a son who goes by that." Then he said, "Imagine how I must feel among friends with names like Donald Justice and Galway Kinnell and W.S. Merwin" — he drew out the syllables, as though he were saying "Rockefeller" and "Vanderbilt" and "DuPont." "Lucky sons-of-bitches, put on earth with poets' names. And here I am, Phil Levine from Detroit." Someone asked about the procedure for applying to the class. He glanced around the room and said, "You look like nice people. You're in."

When I came back the next week, I was a few minutes late and had to climb over other students to an empty seat. Levine stopped talking and looked over at me. "Levine, you schmuck, get here on time," he said. He laughed. It was, I think, the first moment during my time in college that a teacher had addressed me with anything like personal regard. I began writing down everything he said. He wasn't like other professors. He spoke in little jabs, like a boxer, crisp and precise but without any concern for academic refinement. At the beginning of class he bit into an apple and he didn't stop eating until he had consumed the whole thing, core and all. He was blunt and categorical in his statements. He introduced the class to Hemingway's notion of a "shit detector." He pointed to the use of "azure" in a student's poem. "Question: When is the last time you heard the word 'azure'?" A few students fidgeted uncomfortably. "Answer: The last time you did a crossword puzzle." There was something like a collective gasp in the room. We were accustomed to having teachers address us as "the best and the brightest." This was new. About half the students in class were veterans of the college literary scene and seemed to consider themselves members of a vanguard. Levine didn't coddle or equivocate. Fake language made bad poems. He mocked pretension. Another student read aloud her poem in a tone full of silences, exclamations, urgencies. The writer's circle of friends took turns celebrating her. After a pause, Levine spoke. "I heard better language coming over on the bus this morning."

He seemed uninterested in interpreting poems, which was at first mystifying to a student like me, who had been trained to believe that the most valuable response to a poem was finding something clever or unexpected to say about it. He thought that the right words in the right sequence held a power that was magical and instantaneous.

He read poems to us—W.B. Yeats, Thomas Hardy, Wilfred Owen, Elizabeth Bishop—with a passion I had never before encountered. His voice was rough and magisterial. Words were alive in him. He read with a clenched jaw and his body almost shaking. He described John Keats's letters and made clear his sense that the imagination was a sacred place breeding authenticity in words. He insisted that the poem be lived. One student turned in a poem that used the word "lion" a single time, to symbolize power. Levine almost blew up. "Goddamn it," he shouted, "if you're going to put a poor lion in your poem, I want that lion to *be* there." He seemed to hunger after the texture of reality, which took many forms, but which was instantly recognizable to him. Another student's poem began: "A window. A baseball. The possibilities." It was a sparse and, in certain ways, abstract poem. He loved it. He saw a world in it: the object in flight, clean and clear; the suspension of time; the opening of imaginative possibility, of promised lands, however shattered, within the disappointments of the actual one.

Right away, it felt to me that Levine entered my life by the logic of dreams, bringing me to poetry when it was what I most needed, without having any idea I needed it. I had just returned to school following a five-week winter break in Toronto, where I grew up. There was heavy snowfall and bitter cold. My parents were both out of work for health reasons. My father had a spinal injury; my mother had been diagnosed with ovarian cancer the previous spring. They lived in a tiny two-bedroom house they had bought with the hope of enlarging, but construction had stopped when they ran out of money. By then, it was evident my mother's rounds of chemotherapy had been unsuccessful, though the possibility she might die was never discussed. She was forty-nine years old and I was closer to no one. She spent most of that winter break in bed beneath an old afghan in a cramped room whose only window had been boarded over during construction. One night my father took me aside and told me he had noticed a widening crack in a wall. He was certain that the load of snow and ice on the roof was going to lead to the collapse of the house. He told me he didn't want to alarm my mother with the news. Nonetheless, he said, he could think of nothing else. He hadn't slept in weeks.

The first poem I turned in to Levine's class was called "Racing." It started with a memory of racing my mother down the hallway of our apartment building when I was six years old. She would slow down toward the end of the hallway to allow me to arrive at the finish with her. "My mother's days have numbers on them," the poem began. It was full of shrill writing. It had many of the traits I believed poems were required to include: elaborate metaphor, compulsive vividness, heavy-breathing strains of high music. But it also had, it's possible, a trace of the inarticulate desperation I was living with. For a year, I had spoken to no one about my mother's illness, though it dominated my mind throughout every day. I certainly couldn't speak of it to my father. But I had managed, for the first time, to turn to poetry in an effort to specify emotions that were otherwise too harrowing for me to bear or to confront. Some connection I felt with this other Levine — born, uncannily, just a week before my father — had allowed me to do it. I deeply cared what he would say in class. He took the poem seriously. He was kind. He didn't patronize me. He told me what he liked and didn't like. He deflected the criticism of others in the class. He said, "Mr. Levine has work to do, but he has written the first draft of a genuine poem."

He began one class by asking, "Why do you write poetry?" Several students dared to answer. "To make something beautiful" — "To interrogate the dominant ideology" — "To give voice to the powerless." The student with the vinyl fish bag offered, "To get the bug out of my ear." Levine said, "There's only one reason to write poetry. To change the world."

He believed it. He believed poetry was the most important thing a person could do, and that poems bore the impulse for collective transformation without which lies and injustice would prevail. He loathed Reagan. He spoke of the crimes that politicians and capitalists had done to language. The right words mattered, he said, because poems could restore meaning to language. Poems were forbidden from lying.

Did some students find him cruel? Perhaps. His commitment was ferocious. He read aloud a poem by a senior, one of the literary stars of the campus. In Levine's voice, the poem, full of wordplay, ironic jabs, and references to literary theory, sounded spectacular. "Our friend Mr. D. has a flair for language," Levine said. "He's written something very smart, very knowing. It's charismatic and very appealing. It takes pains to show you what a wit the poet is. And if he continues this way, there's a good chance Mr. D. will never write a poem."

Week by week, though, it became clear that Levine was enjoying our group enormously, and the class developed both intimacy and boisterousness. Word got around, and visitors would come to sit in. Most everyone in the room was writing better, more ambitiously, more honestly, and Levine celebrated our small triumphs. He often reminded us how much he preferred us to the graduate students he met immediately after our class. "There's very little talent in that class," he told us. "Last week a student brought in a poem and asked, 'How can I make it better, Phil? How can I make it better?' And I said, 'There's only one way to make it better. Throw it away.'"

He was fifty-seven, but he was not famous and his bearing was embattled. "I didn't find my voice until I was older," he told us. "It was good for me to have the time to work at becoming a poet, and it would be good for you, too. But by the time I was thirty-five and still didn't have a book, I'd had enough, and I was in danger of becoming a real asshole."

Less than halfway through the semester, I returned to Toronto. My mother was in the hospital. I spent the next three weeks in her room. She suffered tremendously. She put up with one monstrous procedure after another in an effort to live marginally longer. I had terrible fights with my father. A stream of visitors came to the room, draining my mother of what energy she had. I had a poem folded in my pocket that I wanted to read to her, but I couldn't find the right moment. Just before she died, as a nurse was struggling to prod a needle into a vein, my mother turned to me and said, "To hell with it."

I returned to school. In the dining hall, prior to Levine's class, I wrote a draft called "Poem For My Birthday, April 17, 1985":

I have shoveled gravel onto our muddy driveway
To keep the mourner's cars from sinking,
Spreading the stones with my old hockey stick.

I brought the poem to class. Levine's presence, his voice, his vision of poetry, had become something of a lifeline for me. After class I went to the bookstore and bought his *Selected Poems* as a birthday present for myself. It was the first book I owned by a living poet. I had never seen such poems: "Baby Villon," "Silent in America," "Animals Are Passing from Our Lives," "Zaydee," "1933." I was overwhelmed. The work was living proof of what I had been hearing in his class: that art could be made out of forceful, hard-won everyday language; that poems didn't have to decide between rage and humor, sorrow and joy; that the imagination gave access to a larger life. I hadn't imagined that one could write poetry as an unapologetic urban Jew — not a tony, long-assimilated German Jew, but one of the more recently arrived, a child of Yiddish-speaking, tenement-dwelling Russian and Polish Jews, shopkeepers and laborers, who didn't have fine manners, who were over-concerned with money, who argued loudly and ate bad food and sometimes got sick and died young and were inconsolable.

A few weeks later, I showed up to the last class. It was a beautiful spring day. Levine was all smiles. "I'm feeling great," he told the group. "I just picked up my paycheck." I brought in a new poem called "My Milieu," about being on vacation with my parents when I was fifteen. "In other times," it began:

> My parents and I woke early
> To eat at a bar,
> A ninety-five cent meal
> On stools.

It was, I think, a hard thing for me to have written, let alone to have brought to class: a poem about being embarrassed by my parents; about being attached to them; about belonging to a family that was gone. The poem ended, "They liked the food,/For them it was/Eating out." My draft of the poem has my handwritten transcription of the class discussion. One student said, reasonably enough, "I don't believe it. It feels pretentious." Another observed, "It's about the relationship of the self to particular societal classes." Levine responded, "What it's about is how difficult it is to live, to live as a young person and then to live as an old person." He recommended I read Rimbaud's "Poet at Seven." He added, "I may be wrong — this poem may be a piece of shit." Several members of the class challenged the poem for its cynicism. Levine interrupted. "You know, people often call my poems cynical," he said. "They say, 'Levine, why are you so damn cynical? Why must you be so cynical?' And I say, 'Fuck you. I'm not being cynical, I'm being realistic.'"

After class, I got my courage up to ask him if we could have a beer together. It wasn't possible that day, he said, but we would find a time to do it soon. He told me I could send him a few poems in the mail when I felt ready to do it. He had given me his honest attention when I needed it, and he would step back and let me be free of his influence when that was called for. It's what one would hope for, but rarely receive, from a teacher or from a parent. A month later I was back in Toronto. It was a difficult time. That June, I received Levine's written evaluation of my classwork. It was a more than generous paragraph. Its last words shocked me — "He could make his mark as a poet" — and changed the course of my life.

JAMES LASDUN

Michael Hofmann

In the early eighties I was employed as one of half a dozen in-house readers at Jonathan Cape, in their old Bedford Square offices. We were all writers and it seemed to be understood that we would spend as much time keeping up with our literary pals as we did reading manuscripts. Poets and novelists would drop in for coffee, or we'd spend hours nattering with them on the phone. Magazine editors would come sniffing around for our latest discoveries. It was like a club within a club, complete with comfy chairs and stacks of periodicals; a last redoubt of gentlemanliness in a profession that hadn't yet, quite, caught up with the rest of the world.

It was Hugo Williams, part of this cozy cabal for a period, who introduced me to Michael Hofmann's poems, which had just begun appearing in the *Times Literary Supplement*. I have to admit I felt stricken by them. I could see at once that they were amazingly good, but also that they were good in ways that were going to have a calamitous effect on all my assumptions about poetry. I'd dismissed the possibility that one could achieve the kind of high-intensity experiences I was looking for in a poem by any other than the most elaborately wrought verbal means. To read these coolly stated, deceptively prose-like poems with their implicit disavowal of anything calculated or orchestrated, their apparent disdain for extended argument or metaphor, and yet feel the same ferocity of emotional and intellectual impact as I found in Yeats and Lowell and Plath, was a disconcerting revelation. It also didn't escape me that this approach opened the poems to aspects of contemporary life — pop, politics, all the dreck and clutter of daily urban existence — that my own methods (such as they were) simply couldn't accommodate, and naturally this added to the general sense of being undone. The coup de grace was that, for all their avoidance of conventional poetic effect, they were ravishingly beautiful pieces of writing; exploding with caustic wit, phosphorescent description, jags of plangent eroticism, and those squalls of weirdly joyous verbal music the like of which, to my knowledge, no one has produced before or since.

Hugo and I and Xandra Hardie convinced our bosses at Cape that we should sign Michael up and we invited him in to the office.

Not surprisingly it turned out Faber were also interested, and it was gloomily understood that he would go there if they made an offer. They did and he went, but it took them a few weeks to come to the decision and by that time our rooms had become a regular port of call on Michael's London peregrinations, and he and I had struck up a friendship.

As with the poems so, at first, with their maker. What initially appealed to me — an unformed, murkily embattled twenty-three-year-old — was his diametric unlikeness to myself; his benign self-possession, global perspective, and air of having long ago figured out what did and did not need to be read, watched, listened to. Everything he thought interested me, and I was still pliable enough in my own views to learn new things and — thank god — unlearn some old ones. I can still hear myself trotting out some remark about poetry being a *craft*, only to be met with a pained furrowing of the brows and pursing of the lips and realizing the utter inadequacy and banality of this position. For a short time I tried imitating his poems — an embarrassing memory comes to me of something full of preemptively resigned lust and knowingly disillusioned politics, all peppered with German and Latin and set in a tube station — but even when I'd realized the futility of this, I continued (and still continue) to find echoes of his highly distinctive tone, syntax, cadences, stylistic tics, in my own prose and poetry. Specific images too, I realize, looking back. Where could the tampon "like a dipstick" in my poem "Buying a Dress" have possibly come from if not the "sparkplugs mixing with tampons" in Michael's "Touring Company"? My appropriations stopped short of the black fedora he wore and the Balkan Sobranies he used to smoke, but a good chunk of his personal canon quickly became incorporated into mine: *Under the Volcano*, *Buddenbrooks*, Musil, Schuyler, Bishop, Iranian movies...

I'm not sure what Michael got from me in return. I probably knew more about food than he did, or cared more, though he's the only thin person I know who can out-eat me, and I've grown fond of his buttery cooking. In terms of literature I think I put him on to Brodsky; later I suppose Ovid. I couldn't persuade him to read Auden properly or Burroughs at all, but I remember him being impressed by the presence of Brecht's poems on my bookshelf, which he took to be the sign of a more cosmopolitan outlook than most English poets had. I don't know if it really was that, but it raises one of the large things we did have in common, which was our uncertain relationship to our own Englishness; complicated by Jewishness on my side and Germanness on his. It wasn't something we talked about at that time but we both surely felt it, and felt drawn to each other because of it.

We also had in common high-achieving, high-visibility fathers; again not something we talked about much, but it deepened the understanding between us, along with the sense of being a little oddly positioned vis-à-vis our own achievements. I suspect it bequeathed us each a bit of an *aut Caesar aut nihil* complex (there, some Latin), which has no doubt caused both of us difficulties at times, but which I like to think we've somewhat overcome, with a little help from each other.

I've been trying to remember those first years of our friendship. Of course I have the singular luxury of needing only to open those first books of Michael's to bring them back: precise details as well as the general atmosphere. We ate long lunches at the Tramontana as per "Fidelity." We went for epic walks around grotty eighties London as per "Nighthawks." In Kensal Green Cemetery we rejoiced to see a gravestone with the name of a poet on it who'd dissed us both. We introduced each other to our mates and sometimes got together en masse — at Stephen and Bridget Romer's house in Senlis, or Geoff Dyer's squat in Brixton, or the Eric Gill/David Jones monastery in Capel-y-ffin that Robin Robertson organized every summer for a while.

We're neither of us great talkers; when we did talk it was more about politics than literature, and possibly more about clothes than politics. Not much about girls (as Hugo once ruefully joked, "he doesn't talk dirty," but then nor do I). When we disagreed about something factual we'd settle it with a bet. In Mexico Michael declared with sublime intransigence that the Mason-Dixon line ran along the Canadian border, and that the flocks of obvious (if rather small) pigeons in Cuernavaca were in fact quail. These rare but striking lapses from omniscience put me in mind of Sherlock Holmes's apparent ignorance of the fact that the earth revolves around the sun. The lacunae became, somehow, further evidence of the genius. And I suspect I am not the only friend of Michael's who feels a little ploddingly Watson-like in his company, or, for that matter, who regards him as something like the Sherlock Holmes of British poetry: preternaturally attuned to reality, somewhat inclined to disappear, and always several leagues ahead of everyone else.

Hayden Carruth

Adrienne Rich was expecting him for lunch at noon, but there was no rushing Hayden. When Jen Richter and I arrived to collect him and his wife, Joe-Anne, at their hotel room, they were sitting with their feet up on the fancy couches, drinking, as though we had no place special to go. It's Adrienne Rich, we reminded Hayden. You know — *the* Adrienne Rich.

Sit down, Joe-Anne said. Have a drink! We'll be ready in a minute.

An hour later we set off from Palo Alto in Jen's red Cabriolet convertible, scurrying across the northern California mountains to the coastal highway and down to Santa Cruz. Hayden, and by extension Jen's little car, smelled of three things: damp tweed, stale tobacco, and Irish whisky. It was 11:45 AM and we were very late. It would take us most of an hour to get to Santa Cruz, slightly less if Jen could take the curves over the mountains with some finesse.

Sitting in the backseat next to Joe-Anne, I contemplated Hayden's hair. It fanned out over the headrest in front of me like a bleached halo: white, with a little yellow. Not a real match for the reddish shade of his mustache and eyebrows. Was his hair, in his youth, once a more reddish color too? Or was his facial hair only this rusty from tobacco smoke? Certainly the cigarette smoke was a constant, engulfing him every hour of every day. It was easy to imagine the extent to which his facial hair had absorbed the stain, as had the index and middle fingers of his right hand, each marked with a deep mustard ovoid where he gripped his cigarettes.

Remember that? When people smoked?

White-haired, red-haired: he looked crazy old, and also just plain crazy: the top of his head nearly bald; the rest of his hair growing amply, eyebrows sprouting exuberant sprongs, beard so bushy it concealed his mouth, the hair on his head growing so long and shaggy that it reached nearly to his shoulders, puffing up around his head and over his ears, eternally tousled, a halo, a mane, a cotton swab. I peered closer. Underneath its layers, I could now see, some remnant black lurked. So the hair was never red.

When you looked at Hayden dead-on you saw first that wild hair. Next, his peering eyes, gray-blue, cloudy with cataracts, nearly

disappearing behind those magnificent eyebrows and the deep crin-
kles that erupted whenever he giggled, which, surprisingly, was often,
given how fierce he at first seemed. Hayden's habit as it turned out,
in addition to the cigarettes, was telling tales — then instantly laughing at them as hard as anyone, or even if no one else laughed. He told
these tales in public, in crowds, among friends; told them, apparently,
whenever he felt anxious, or shy, or disgruntled, or amused.

For several days, Hayden had been the guest of the Stegner
Fellowship program at Stanford University — three days of continuous
socializing, meeting people who brought with them an expectation
that he would make articulate and observable in some meaningful
way the solitary activity of writing poetry. This cannot be an easy
thing for anyone to do, especially for a man who for a period of years
had been severely agoraphobic, "tormented by a fear of people and
open spaces," as William Grimes wrote in Hayden's *New York Times*
obituary: unable even to leave his own house, much less interact with
strangers. With Hayden, long moments of self-conscious silence,
during which he seemed entirely unable to participate in the ongoing
conversation, would be suddenly broken by the recounting of one
of these tales, or by sudden blurts of rhyme, perhaps an old Billie
Holiday song, altered to suit his ear, seemingly apropos of nothing
but some dialogue taking place within his head — *Our love is a faucet*,
he chanted in the hotel lobby,

> It's either off or on.
> Just when I think it's on,
> Baby, it's off and gone.

Together with his bed-rumpled appearance, this survivalist behav-
ior could be off-putting. One could see it strike a mild alarm in the
eyes of people who maybe hadn't yet read his poems or maybe had
read them but failed to get them. The sponsors of the event, generous
though they were, had looked at Hayden when they first met him as
though they'd unwittingly invited in Dr. Strangelove, gleefully rid-
ing his nuclear missile to their mutual devastation. "'I wish I could
shimmy like my sister Kate,'" Hayden told us. "'She shakes it like
jelly on a plate.'"

•

The main event had taken place the previous evening, a reading of his poems that Hayden had given before a packed house, and this day, heading down to Adrienne Rich's for lunch, would be his last in town. His relief was evident. This was why he had needed to lounge about the hotel room for a while, feeling his freedom, re-gathering his strength; it didn't mean he didn't want to see Adrienne. Hayden and Adrienne, we had learned, were old friends — I mean *old* friends. She was someone with whom he could be utterly relaxed. She would forgive him his tardiness. For although Hayden and his wife both clearly liked Jen and me, we were new acquaintances. We were his minders.

Our initial duty had been to take Hayden and Joe-Anne out for a fancy meal on their first evening in town. At the table, before he even sat down, Hayden shifted his water glass over to Joe-Anne, saying, "You know I don't drink this stuff."

He meant the water. "He says fish fuck in it," Joe-Anne explained.

Joe-Anne was considerably younger than Hayden, with striking, long red hair, and her devotion — and his to her — was absolute. It is difficult to imagine how he would have functioned without her. On the day of his public reading, he had set out in the morning on a long walk and quickly become lost, wandering "fourteen miles," as he described it, although how he eventually found his way home to the campus hotel he wasn't sure. Along the way he'd asked for help, and this was where the tale began to sound epically Hayden: he'd asked everyone where the Faculty Club was, a place unknown to most citizens of Silicon Valley. In his baggy, stained trousers and limp cotton shirt, his long hair uncombed, a cigarette pinched between his fingers, he was an unlikely figure on the streets of one of the most expensive towns in the country. I have to read my poems, he told strangers. Where is the Faculty Club? The man at the information desk in the mall blinked rapidly and shook his head. On the street, several people refused to answer him, edging nervously away, until finally, on the Stanford Campus itself, a policeman told him, "You don't belong here." In the range of creatures that Hayden might apparently be, no one had guessed what they were actually dealing with.

"Poems," Hayden said that night, "are mushrooms cropping up under a leaf, growing on that log. Some are very tasty and some could kill you."

Over the three days of his visit, Jen and I had gradually felt Hayden lower his invisible force field until he seemed actually glad to see us. If this meant hanging out in his hotel room and being late for Adrienne

Rich, well, so be it. And it was hard to be worried when it was such a gorgeous drive down the coast. Jen showed finesse, and we made good time. When the car pulled up at the curb, Jen beeped the horn at Hayden's request and soon the front door swung open to show the famous woman we had seen photos of, whose poems we had cut our teeth on, but never imagined we would meet. She smiled and waved, betraying no annoyance whatsoever that Hayden was late.

We were meant just to be dropping Hayden and Joe-Anne off, but Adrienne insisted we join them for the meal. She wouldn't let us refuse and we didn't try too hard. After lunch, since smoking was not allowed inside the house, Hayden wandered off into Adrienne's backyard to have a cigarette or two while we cleared the table. We offered to wash the dishes. We tried very hard to wash Adrienne Rich's dishes, but she refused our help, pretended she would save them for later, and shooed us outside to find Hayden before he could get himself lost. As we slipped out the kitchen's glass door, she was standing at the sink, washing the dishes.

Adrienne's back porch was much larger than it had at first appeared: it only began outside the kitchen door and then, after a corner, wrapped around the entire back of the house as though designed for large parties around a pool. Yet we could not imagine Adrienne hosting a pool party. Then we rounded the corner and came upon not cabanas and wicker lounges, but a hundred or so individual assorted cacti in numerous pots, each distinctly individual from spine to ceramic base, all arranged as though with some bird's-eye design in mind — careful still-lives with various porous bits of wood and stones of some interest, including one with a deep fossilized impression of a fern.

Of Hayden there was no sign.

"He'll be lost again," Joe-Anne said, with mild concern.

We headed out of the yard and down the scrub-lined street, the hot sun bearing down from a textureless blue sky, and it was some time before we finally spotted him, his back to us as he shuffled along. He looked as though he might just keep on going, wherever the road went, apparently aimless, yet dogged, and therefore with some purpose, like the hitching rhythm of my favorite Hayden poem —

> Hey, hey, daddio,
> Them old jeans is
> Going to go!

Rose Marie done put in a new
Valve cover gasket,
Them jeans good for a whole nother
10,000 mile ...
— From *November Jeans Song*

Jen shouted, "Hey, good-looking!" and Hayden spun toward us, delight on his face, his cigarette suspended in his fingers and perched near the corner of his mouth.

I look back upon the scene from these many years later at the breathing image of the man not so long gone, walking down the street near the home of another poet, also now gone: I might imagine I see King George, or a homeless vagrant, or Walt Whitman, shuffling past the neat adobe ranches of that quiet suburb in northern California. The sun was hot. The sky, blue. We stepped up to collect Hayden Carruth, laughing in the street, and returned him to Adrienne, who was waiting in her house with tea.

How it is never the same
but always changing. How
sometimes nevertheless
you recognize it. How you
see it from your window
plunging down, flattening
across the frozen lawn,
then rising in a wild
swirl and it's gone ...
— From *Woodsmoke at 70*

A FEW MORE DON'TS

Ezra Pound set forth his now-famous "A Few Don'ts by an Imagiste" in the March 1913 issue of Poetry. *In commemoration we've asked a few writers to update Pound's essay for our time. Four appear here with others following next month.*

No more

No more lines on the luminescence of light, of whatever variation.
No more elegies of youth or age, no polyglottal ventriloquism.
No more songs of raw emotion, forever overcooked.
No more the wisdom of banality, which should stay overlooked.
No more verbs of embroidery.
No more unintentional phallacy.
No more metaphor, no more simile. Let the thing be, concretely.
No more politics put politically: let the thing be concretely.
No more conditional set conditionally — let the thing be already.
No more children pimped out to prove some pouting mortality.
No more death without dying — *immediately*.
No more poet-subject speaking into the poem-mirror, watching
    the mouth move, fixing the thinning hair.
No more superiority of the interiority of that unnatural trinity —
    you, me, we — our teeth touch only our tongues.
No more Gobstoppers: an epic isn't an epic for its fingerprints.
No more reversals of grammar *if as* emphasis.
No more nature less natural; no more impiety on bended knee.
No more *jeu de mot*, no more *mot juste*.
No more retinal poetry.

JOSHUA MEHIGAN

Make Make It New New

Asked to compile a list of proscriptions, à la Pound, I was a little worried. My first impulse was to try to be funny. Then I started a project
that involved reading thousands of pages of new, unpublished poetry.
That put me in a more thoughtful and serious mood. It was as if all the
young poets had been told beforehand what six or seven qualities would
be rewarded and had gone charging after those alone. It comes down to
a straining for effect. This is nothing new. But that's part of the point.

   As usual everything is all about a kind of unusualness. There's ordinary sensationalism, as when the word anus or the word hegemon
suddenly appears in a poem about a bowl of fruit. There's uncon-
ventional typography: the italic voice-from-the-beyond, secret in-
dentation systems, banished punctuation, etc. But there is also a new,
relentless infatuation with whimsical discontinuity. One tactic is obscurity, which may include nonsequential thinking, ellipsis, or dreamlike imagery. Obscurity can be wild (Breton), atmospheric (Bishop),
or imitative of thought (Eliot). It can reward you with a mindblowing
revelation (Dickinson). But the obscurity I've encountered recently is
merely outlandish, and unyielding. It vibrates with the superficiality
of fashion: there is nothing better for it to do but stand there being
cute and empty. Non sequiturs abound, in two main flavors, quirkily
funny and very — so very — serious. Undemanding punch-line-style
ironies are everywhere, and so are Bland Statements of Profundity.
In an important subtype, mock-profundity replaces profundity, with
a result probably meant to sound like Ashbery or James Tate. Often
the best you can hope for in this kind of poem is a hollow cleverness
that might be termed "a wonderfully skewed perspective." Part of
this is how much a matter of course poets have made nonconformism. The automatic reduplication of provocative gestures is dulling.
The field becomes more and more homogeneous, the sameness cam-
ouflages whatever good hides there, and poets continue winking as
if they were devastatingly original. Poetry becomes another variety
of conformist nonconformism, like Green Day or ironic eyewear.

   Commemorating Pound may be what brought him to my mind.
But it's no accident that he stuck there like a radio jingle. After all,
what are these offputting tendencies if not the *reductio ad absurdum*

of Modernism? Each is marked by cargo-cult qualities cultivated by Pound, such as novelty, imaginative priority, fragmentation, and difficulty. All of these are desirable sometimes, one or two most of the time. But the special formulae popularized by the Modernists and their followers provide what must be the most brutally contrived models younger poets have ever had to start from.

You can't hold the Modernists solely responsible. They may've wanted to install themselves as oracles of some final indestructible -ism, but they invented no new poetic first principles. Few young poets name Pound as a main influence, and many now get their Williams and Stevens from later poets, in the way half the country gets its water from soda pop or beer. However we come to it, Modernism is always there, and apparently we haven't yet begun the process that leads to our having detested it long enough.

Literary movements often exhaust themselves before their last adherents notice. But these days it's like being on a crowded escalator when the people at the top step off and stop dead. Modernism is an especially hard case because of the specific character of its most celebrated principles and the hard-line approach of its leaders, many of whom could've bullied Bill O'Reilly down to the size of a Pekingese. Of course Modernism is complex, but its leaders hammered up its most revolutionary points with evangelical zeal. Its campaign for novelty and iconoclasm continues clearing space for pioneers like Rothko, or the Stooges, or Béla Tarr. But, after awhile, oversupply does what it does and devalues the new coinage. Novelty gets rarer, no icons are left to smash, and nothing is more predictable than whimsy.

Modernism also stirs up a lower-stakes version of the us-and-them dichotomy of authoritarian regimes. Opponents are ignored or ridiculed, and any alternative to acceptable practice is sweepingly dismissed as cliche — the cold kiss of death in all arts. Meanwhile, Modernist cliches go unrecognized because they are cliches of Modernism, enemy of all cliches.

In the end, poetry looks radical only to the outside world, which ignores it, while from inside it looks static. Poets got out of these situations before by doing something new, but novelty is superfluous now. There is no way to get into the game without upping the ante, and there is no way out without bluffing or folding or everyone agreeing on a new game. If you've been a poet for a while you might not see how bizarre it all seems, and how monotonous, but if you shake your head and look again as a human being, you might.

REGINALD DWAYNE BETTS

What It Is

This ain't about risk. Risk is living below the poverty line in the worst part of town; risk is raising a black boy in a town with laws like Stand Your Ground; risk is being a single parent without family or community support; risk is what soldiers, police officers, firefighters encounter. Poetry is about language, words, about being as honest as you can on the page.

There are things you say in a room with friends. Things you hear others say and can't forget, 'cos you spent an hour arguing with them, or laughing. The poem should be that, something worth screaming about.

Don't forget Yeats. Respond to the political in all its ambiguity because you know the people who died, not because you caught the highlights on the news.

Don't write about being white.

Don't be afraid to hate poems. Don't be afraid to hate your own.

There are no large issues in America outside of race. Derek Walcott said this. If you're writing and not thinking of race, you're still thinking of race by avoiding it.

Don't be the person who only notices the elephant in the room.

Don't believe them when they say a poem has room for everything. Only the grave does.

Stop with the allusions to dead poets. You do something other than read poetry.

Don't be the poet who, ensconced in your 401(k) and tenure track, dismisses the man on the corner selling his work, fresh from Kinkos — he could be Whitman.

I keep arguing about vernacular. What it is, what it means. Who has a right to it. For real I'm confronting the fact that I lost all the slang of my youth in my youth. The poem is the only way I have of getting it back.

Don't betray the people you right about.

Don't believe the reviewer who wrote: "I am not sure it is possible for a Negro to write well without making us aware he is a Negro; on the other hand, if being a Negro is the only subject, the writing is not important."

Don't strip your poem of identity. Don't make your identity the poems.

Pay homage, but if the illest thing about your poem is your litany of influences, you wrote a bibliography. Call it that.

Don't feel too bad about that last line.

Right now there is someone lying to a child, praising the work of some thirteen-year-old kid as if it were the sign of latent genius. Don't be that person. Teaching poetry to children isn't about discovering genius. It's about discovering language, and discovering the difficulties inherent in manipulating it.

Don't walk into an underserved classroom imagining that the poems the kids write will replace all that they aren't learning. Don't front like poems are born out of experiences and not the reckless wrestling with nouns and verbs and all the other engines of language.

Work in a place where no one knows what an iamb is.

Don't condescend. There is prejudice in calling something beautiful for the act and not the fact.

The colloquial is always musical. "You lucky I can't breathe or I'd walk all up and down your ass."

JILL ALEXANDER ESSBAUM

A Poem Should Not Be Mean But Behave:
Good Breeding for Poems

The difference though, between letter-writers of the past and of the present, is that
in other days they all tried to write, and to express themselves the very best they
knew how — to-day people don't care a bit whether they write well or ill.
— Emily Post, Etiquette in Society, in Business, in Politics and at Home, *1922*

CONCERNING DRESSES AND STRESSES

Fashion and beauty have little in common, though fashion has wiles
enough to mimic what's beautiful.

A remarkable hat will not suffice when paired with a hideous ensem-
ble. Never waste a peerless title on a frumpy or unkempt poem. The
inverse of this rule also applies.

The woman of irreproachable style will always veer slightly from
current fashion. The poem of genuine brilliance will be consistently
misconstrued.

When in doubt, choose the plainer dress, the simpler word.

Beware of faddism, flummery.

How dashing, a tuxedo tailored to fit! What elegance, the made-to-
measure gown! In the matter of formal poetry, the practice of altering
a traditional pattern to achieve an exclusive, inimitable fit is customary.
Here, a (hem) line taken in. There, a qua(train) added on. For, as the
simple rhyme instructs us: *When garment of poetry bespoke be / Your*
verse shall be spoken most radiantly!

The best suit is always the one that suits best the body that wears it.

TABLE GRACES: WHAT'S REPAST IS PROLOGUE

A metaphor is not an oyster fork, a utensil to be employed on rare and singular occasions. Sonic tension isn't a pair of sugar tongs, a tool for teatime alone. Image, language, sound. *Napkin, plate, knife.* Regular, usual implements of the table.

Never pour gravy on an empty plate nor heap flourish upon the vacant husk of a poem.

Let no guest wait long for his meat. Linger not over opening lines. Proceed with main course and poem alike lest shoulder of lamb turn cold ... *and even colder shoulder of reader be given.*

Do not rush to eat the epicure's meal. Never give cursory eye to a luminous poem.

Prepare neither banquet nor ballad in haste. It is rude to the process of both.

It is permissible to eat the peach.

TO FEEL A FUNERAL

Grief: *A universal undertaking experienced by one's Self.*

Poetry: *An appall bearer.*

All sorrow is sacred. The necessity for dignity cannot be over-emphasized.

Can you see well enough to write in deepest darkness? No? *Write anyway.*

WITH RUDE MY HEART IS LADEN: A MISCELLANY OF POETIC COURTESY

Never interrupt a conversation. Don't speak when a poem is speaking to you.

Honor thy father and mother. Learn the contemporary classics.

When witty, refrain from self-congratulation. Insufferable are they who titter at their own bon mots.

The well-bred poem is neither loquacious nor reticent, neither garrulous nor muttering.

A lounging demeanor telegraphs lassitude. Poem: *Stand up!*

WHEN TWO ROADS DIVERGE

Obey no rule that impedes good art.

COMMENT

JASON GURIEL

Autobiography of Reader

Red Doc>, by Anne Carson.
Alfred A. Knopf. $24.95.

The first thing I notice, flipping through the new Anne Carson, is
fancy lining: the Canadian poet and classicist has center-justified the
bulk of the text, leaving it to the word processor (not for the first
time a collaborator) to work out the spacing — and leaving a strip of
aerated text down the middle of most pages. Is this poetry? Prose?
Like other recent Carson productions, *Red Doc>,* the sequel to 1998's
verse novel *Autobiography of Red,* is a feast for first glances.

But when I resolve finally to turn away from surface pleasures and
reckon with the words, I encounter nothing less than the voice of,
well, Anne Carson! — learned, deadpan, comma-less, and frequently
carried away by tangent. In other words, I encounter page after page
of this:

> GATHERING   SWIM
> GEAR in the bathroom he
> glances   at   the   mirror.
> Sharp   stab   his   face   no
> longer   young   no   more
> beauty   impact.   Get   used
> to   this.   Other   ways   to
> navigate   the   world.   Did
> Daniil   Kharms   have   this
> particular   rug   pulled   out
> from   under   him   one   day   in
> a   bathroom   in   Leningrad   it
> seems unholy to ask.

A consistent, distinctive voice isn't usually a problem. (Most poets
should be so lucky.) But I'm not very far into *Red Doc>* when I find
myself wondering why a voice so unperturbed by its latest packaging — long and short lines, rival columns, the screenplay, the essay,
opera — needed such packaging in the first place. It's hard to think

of another more restless poet, whose adventures in form and genre, from book to book, have left less of a mark on her sensibility. Is it that the medium isn't so much the message as the marketing strategy? Carson poems, I'm convinced, will soon come packaged in a Cornell box — but they will sound like Carson.

I'm also not very far in when I find myself wondering what's going on. Already I'm leaning far too much on a rather slim crutch, near to buckling: the advance copy's blurb. It explains that Geryon, the red-winged monster from *Autobiography of Red*, has reached manhood and now goes by "G" (we should be grateful; a savvier poet, sensing an opportunity, would've selected the Twitter handle "@Geryon"). The blurb also identifies some of the supporting characters and their professions (artist, war veteran). This is most helpful; pronouns in *Red Doc>* don't always have obvious owners, and dramatic dialogue doesn't always earn the backslashes the poet seems to feel are sufficient to parse the speakers. Indeed, doesn't this rapid-fire deadpanning between Ida (the artist) and Sad (the war veteran) —

why'd you
enlist / oh people thought
I'd be better off / off / I was
getting into mischief /
people

like who / Dad / mischief
like what / is this an
interview / I like to close all
the loops /

— sound a lot like this rapid-fire, deadpanning between G and one Lieutenant M'hek —

you're the
team /

small team / you're the
guy who comes every
evening with the drugs /
no my team is
nonpsychotropic / so

what do you do / talk /
does that help him / one
test for this question /
what test / did he cap
himself yesterday /

Are these the voices of four characters talking? — or is Carson merely in talks with herself?

Far scarier than keeping the characters straight: the blurb hints that *Red Doc>* is "haunted by Proust." Carson books typically have truck with an intertext or two, and I typically do OK. I know enough about *Wuthering Heights*, Keats, Duchamp, and the like to have gotten by in the past. But Proust? I empathize with G's mom who, early in *Red Doc>*, declares, "well I'm//not fond of those multivolume things" and "[it] could be too late for me to appreciate Proust on/the other hand I'm at a loss/I've read all the Len//Deightons in the library." *Oh, moms and their middlebrows!* Carson's text seems to sigh. But I empathize with G's; this review is her autobiography, too.

•

I want to write something like, "When last we left Geryon, he was lighting out for the territories" — but *Autobiography of Red* wasn't that kind of book, with characters you especially cared about and a hairpin plot to organize them. It was more a weave of loose ends: set pieces in which an arty teenager lives among humans who aren't terribly concerned he's a red monster out of myth. (To wit: his mother "neaten[s] his little red wings" before sending him "through the door.") In one kind of early Carson poem, the past exerts its pressures on the present; for instance, *Wuthering Heights* weighs on a forlorn woman. In another kind, the past breaks cleanly through; Hektor writes his wife from the set of a TV shoot. *Red* was the cartoony culmination of that other kind of poem. The original Geryon is slain for his herd by Herakles (or Hercules); Carson's mythic red monster goes to school, works a library's stacks, pines for Herakles (now more asshole than hero), inscribes postcards with "bits of Heidegger," and produces an autobiography in "the form/of a photographic essay" — begun, as such things are these days, at a young age (five!). Think highbrow *Hellboy*, and you're not far off; *Red* would've appealed to a readership aging out of an enthusiasm for Anne Rice or

Neil Gaiman and into seminars on deconstruction, queer theory, and classical mythology. It even came equipped with an apparatus of playful scholarship — grad school made cool. But the cover's cursive ("A Novel in Verse") and strategic stain (suggesting the book had been steeped in Earl Grey) called out to old souls everywhere.

In a verse novel of moments, some of *Autobiography of Red*'s were masterfully engaging, but only to the extent that they made an original observation (a new simile, say) with precision: "Passengers streamed/on board like insects into lighted boxes and the experiment roared off down the street." Other, less visionary moments, however, were conspicuously opaque:

> The instant of nature
> forming between them drained every drop from the walls of his life
> leaving behind just ghosts
> rustling like an old map.

Was that mixed drink of a metaphor, layered over four lines, the sort of thing Michael Ondaatje was drunk on when he announced, "Anne Carson is, for me, the most exciting poet writing in English today"? Was Ondaatje, a master of overwriting himself, anointing a successor?

Carson is too successful to be condescended to; she doesn't need my help. But the autobiography of any reader will betray its weak spots, moments of humanity (or vanity) in which the reader wishes he could protect the author from, well, all her other readers! Some of these enablers — otherwise reasonable critics — defend Carson's unevenness. "If a good line happens, it happens," wrote Guy Davenport back in the nineties. "What you get is the over-all action of the mind rather than the high-shine lacquer of the apt image," wrote Meghan O'Rourke in 2010. Carson as uncooked savant — that's one way of explaining away the longeur between her better lines. It also establishes two bars of commitment: a low one for the poet (who's an innocent anyway, a flake adrift on her breeziness, on autopilot) and a high one for the reader (who should be grateful merely for the work of interpreting the innocent's utterances). If *Autobiography of Red* didn't present Carson's best (that would be the *Wuthering Heights* poem), it did provide, as commercial successes will do, a version of Carson that's convenient to recall: uneven, but daringly — necessarily — so. It takes slightly more effort to imagine a poet who can capture the insects in lighted boxes, but who can't keep (or won't abide) an editor to corral her other, flightier impulses.

•

A particularly amiable group of misfits has gathered itself around G, now a mature herdsman of musk oxen. Carson has headhunted the quirkier elements of some quad: these include Sad (the aforementioned war veteran, who seems to have PTSD), Ida (the artist, who takes no shit), 4NO (some guy who thinks he's a god), and Io (an ox who will get high on a hallucinogen and take flight with G — monster's best friend). As in *Autobiography of Red*, the characters live from set piece to set piece. Nothing else — such as voices of their own — conspires to give them life. By *Red Doc>*'s midpoint, some of the misfits have made fast friends, observed oxen, and traveled to a glacier. The text takes occasional, scholarly sidebar to hash out the nature of polar exploration, the principles of flight, the role of oxen in military history. Near the glacier is another chilly place: a psychiatric clinic where G's entourage holes up for a time and encounters authority figures like CMO, which would seem to be short for "Chief Medical Officer." This particular cartoon (Ida calls him "Pig Doc") "laughs/horribly" and believes in, natch:

> Rationality.
> Principle of order. A
> prescribed amount at a
> prescribed time. It's how
> you keep animals in line it
> works for people too.

When we first meet CMO, he is fixing a car. Will the menacing mechanic also try to fix the minds of G and co.?

For every gleamingly exact image in *Red Doc>* —

> Each [ox] head
> has two horns that part as
> neatly as a boy about to
> play the piano wets his
> hair and hopes it stays
> flat for the whole recital.

—there are many more vague, unrealized ones:

> A LITTLE ZIPPER whine
> that runs along the
> convolutes of his ear
> licking in under every
> bone like a bad emotion.

"Night's bones are still/forming"; "A/bright smell streams into/the car"; "the entire/cold sorrow acre of human/history." Of course, I'm over the moon for crescent-crisp similes like "The moonlit/ironing boards/grandstanding like steeds." And I'm all for economical solutions like "He sits/up suddenly drenched in/ringing. Phone." But what do we make of a book that also finds room for the following: "His/heart sinks"; "stop on a dime"; "her nerves are/already tingling"; "right on/the money"; "come at her with/murder in his black eyes"; "who had/the heart"; "a smile that/dazzles"; "a stab of envy"; "clean as a/whistle." Surely even a daringly uneven talent shouldn't be permitted as many cliches as Carson is?

•

Halfway through the book, I seem to be getting by without the background in Proust. I'm sure I'm missing resonances; but Carson has assumed I share enough of her knowledge to ask a rhetorical question, while also ensuring the reference, if it escapes me, is self-explanatory:

> What a scamp that Proust.
> That Albertine. Does
> anyone really believe the
> girl stays asleep for four
> pages in volume v while
> Marcel roams around her
> prostrate form and
> stretches out beside it on
> the bed.

Other kindred souls — that flapper-era reader of *The Waste Land*, say — didn't have it half as good. (Can you imagine Eliot deigning to clarify themes in the colloquial: "What a mess this modern world.

That fisher king. Does anyone really believe the scamp can make the thing rosy again?") Is this, then, part of Carson's appeal — she allows amateurs a little bit of light contact with literature they might not otherwise read? Those of us who don't have our Proust have already been encouraged to identify with G's well-meaning mom. If we press on to the end of the section, we discover that the sleeping girl, prostrate in the eyes of Proust, is "a sleep plant that/cannot tell him lies or/ escape his knowing. Poor/Marcel. What is there to/know." Not much, it turns out. I don't need to lug around "multivolume things"; I just need to linger a little in a seminar on the male gaze.

To what extent is Proust — or Beckett, or whomever a Carson book recruits — an interchangeable signifier of hefty, high culture? Discussing the typical Paul Auster novel, James Woods elegantly describes the maneuver: "A visiting text — Chateaubriand, Rousseau, Hawthorne, Poe, Beckett — is elegantly slid into the host book." Whom, I've started to wonder, will Carson host next? What is there to quote?

•

In one scene of *Autobiography of Red*, gazing out a car window, young Geryon "thought about thoughts." Is Carson's ideal reader the sort of person who enjoys the thought that he or she is the sort of person who thinks about thinking?

•

In the latter half of *Red Doc>*, Carson's misfits help put on a play, spring one of their own from the clinic, and pick up by the side of the road — who else? — Hermes in a "silver tuxedo." A slightly stiff lieutenant, a colleague of Sad's, pitches in and learns to tend oxen (and, I suppose, his soft, springy side; instead of being pilfered by some violent hero, some Herakles, the herd is seen to). Someone always seems to be weeping in *Red Doc>*: "G weeps/thinking of Proust"; "[Sad] weeps in a sort of fury"; "[Sad] starts to cry"; "Tears pour in Ida's/heart"; "[G] grips/his arm and weeps"; "The/weeping has been arriving/about every seven/minutes." Is it that characters who are types are typically given to tears? Carson's are given to breaking into song, waltz. They find themselves befriended by bats, who swoop in to lend a wing, the way small critters will do at cartoon's crescendo. Their antecedents would seem to be J.D. Salinger's Glass family, Wes Anderson's moody prodigies — creative, misunderstood souls. Ida, for one, "often gets lost in basements well in fact Ida often gets lost. Despite map or compass." I would expect no less than aimlessness from Carson's right-brained heroes.

And then there's G, already an autobiographer, about whom the text observes:

> Writing itself is what he
> loves now the mental
> action the physical action.
> He thinks about writing all
> the time while doing other
> things or talking to people
> he is forming sentences in
> his head it keeps the white
> away.

In the life of every reader comes a moment, maybe several, when he thinks, hey, maybe he should try his hand at poems. But passages like the above are insidious to the extent that they portray writing as painless, pleasurable "action." "I hate writing, I love having written," said Dorothy Parker, who had the love-hate balance about right. The genius of G's ongoing saga — and surely one reason for the first book's success — is the silent appeal it makes to the alienated adolescent in all of us: we, too, can be memoirists of our own monstrosity. We would be better off heeding Elizabeth Bishop's observation: "it's true, children sometimes write wonderful things, paint wonderful pictures, but I think they should be *dis*couraged." We would be better off clipping G's wings.

•

In the last act, G arrives at his mother's deathbed, and the reader arrives at the best writing in all of *Red Doc>*. It may be that a person starved for verse is primed to receive even the slightest noise as music — but Carson has written beautifully about parents before: "The Glass Essay," "Father's Old Blue Cardigan," *The Beauty of the Husband*. Here, she writes so well about G's dying mother, you wonder why she felt she needed the preceding picaresque, the Proust-

dropping, the oxing around. Check out, instead, Carson's eleventh
hour meditation on time, a poignant page of doggerel on mothers,
and these other, assorted epiphanies:

> WHEN HE IS there they
> lift the stones together.
> The stones are her lungs.

> •

> How
> strange his mother is lying
> out there in her little
> soaked Chanel suit.

> •

> At home they
> all seemed caught in a
> badly blocked play and
> faces put on wrong.

Were this a true autobiography of reader (and not what it actually
is: broadsides of book reviewer), I would've bailed on *Red Doc>* the
moment Io, in flight, "lets loose a great fart and poops gloriously just
missing [G's] head." That was the real end of me. The death of the
reader. But given the nature of the gig, I had to resurrect my resolve
and push onward; I had no choice. Those who *have* the choice may
wonder, not unreasonably, whether a few late fragments — that hint
at some better book, set at a hospital: *Red at a Death Bed* — are worth
their effort. It's a valid question, though one that probably doesn't
occur much to classicists. Or archaeologists. Or the sort of person
who takes solace in a scene that would seem to be about Proust but is,
in fact, about a much more Sisyphean figure — the Anne Carson fan:

> this lost city
> whose smashed clues and
> indecipherable evidence
> poor Marcel has to dig
> through each evening

feverish for a real shard.
How was your day? this
question on which so much
hangs. You don't really
want to know. Yet he
keeps digging.

JEFFREY YANG

Translating the Abyss

I used to keep a list of books in which "the abyss" appeared — the physical-metaphorical-metaphysical-condition-of-the-bottomless-existence-of-our-darkest-nightmares-realized abyss. The Biblical abyss of formlessness, darkness, apocalypse, and hell; the ordinary abyss that is our "daily routine," as Mexican poet Rosario Castellanos saw it in Silvina Ocampo's poems; "the salutary sense of the abyss that yawns for everyone who has embraced the literary profession," as Canadian poet John Glassco puts it.

In September 1866, Emerson writes in his journal, "There may be two or three or four steps, according to the genius of each, but for every seeing soul there are two absorbing facts, — *I and the Abyss.*" In the *Rig Veda*, the circa twelfth century BC collection of Sanskrit hymns that is scripture for Hindus, one refrain is translated by Wendy Doniger as: "Sky and earth, guard us from the monstrous abyss." In this prayer, sky and earth are deities and understood as either two sister goddesses or as father and mother of the sun, which in a different verse is called "the poet of space." The Sanskrit word translated as "abyss" Doniger notes as *abhvam*, "a dark, formless, enormous and terrifying abyss, particularly associated with night and the underworld, and hence opposed to the light of the worlds of sky and earth." *Abhvam* is also one name for the rift that forms the Sunda Strait between the islands of Java and Sumatra. Deep in the abysses of the sea, the cephalopod *Vampyroteuthis infernalis* dwells in its *umwelt*, so that Vilém Flusser can write, as translated by Valentine A. Pakis, "The vampyroteuthis has forsaken the protection of a shell and can hold itself upright thanks only to the pressure at the bottom of the sea. The price that humans had to pay is the protection bestowed by the ground, by the floor; its price is banishment into the abyss, to be pressed against the deepest floor of all. We are estranged from the earth, and it from the sky. Analogous alienations."

Sky and earth, guard us from the monstrous abyss.

My list of the abyss grew and grew, until I eventually grew tired of it in the realization that the abyss was everywhere (at the edge of nowhere). I decided to leave it to memory to trigger and filter what I would remember of my literary abysses, like Old MacDonald on his farm, with a Baudelaire here and a Nietzsche there, here an Ungaretti, there a Saint Teresa, everywhere a Kafka ... I even lost the list (not deliberately), and yet certain entries burned even brighter in my mind, like Edmond Jabès writing through Rosmarie Waldrop's translation: "You will follow the book, whose every page is an abyss where the wing shines with the name." Such lines breathe the air and light. *Sky and earth, guard us from the monstrous abyss.*

I recall that a large chunk of my lost list yawned across great swathes of Latin America — the Chilean Roberto Bolaño being particularly abyssian. For a dozen years I've worked as an editor at his first us publisher, and I've read each of his books as they came to press, or often before. This was one reason why he figured so prominently on my list, and why a genius like the schizophrenic Cuban, Guillermo Rosales, who disappeared into the halfway houses of Miami, appeared (and could be cross-referenced with a different, very long, and, alas, also lost list of writers who immigrated to America and committed suicide, like the Hungarian Sándor Márai, who shot himself in the head in his apartment near the San Diego Zoo. In his novel *The Rebels*, Márai says through George Szirtes: "And if you write something down, is it then lost, does it have nothing to do with you any more, is there only a memory, an ache, left behind, as if you had been found guilty of something, something for which, sooner or later, you would have to answer?"). And yet one can say that the labyrinth is to Borges what the abyss is to Bolaño — a radiating depth that verges on a cliche. Bolaño must have felt the abyss in the marrow of his bones, to the point of obsession, or perhaps of possession. For him, another word for "abyss" could be "hell," sometimes "Latin America," or "poetry," or "literature," or rather the "abyss of literature," or more specifically, as he writes in *Distant Star*, "literature's bottomless cesspools." At one moment in his novel, translated by Chris Andrews and which Bolaño describes elsewhere as a "modest approximation of absolute evil," the narrator, arrested for his anti-Pinochet activities, watches from a prison courtyard as the fascist poet Carlos Wieder sky-writes in a Messerschmitt 109 fighter plane the opening lines of Genesis in Latin, "IN PRINCIPIO ... CREAVIT DEUS ... CÆLUM ET TERRAM.... ET TENEBRAE ... SUPER FACIEM ABYSSI ...," ending with "ET DIVISIT ... LUCEM AC TENEBRAS" ... learn. The abyss, Bolaño reminds us, has existed from the beginning; it is in every beginning — with emptiness and the Spirit moving across the waters of the earth — before light, before dawn.

Sky and earth, guard us from the monstrous abyss.

Two essays in Bolaño's *Between Parentheses*, translated by Natasha Wimmer, are titled "Our Guide to the Abyss" and "A Stroll Through the Abyss": the first is about *Huckleberry Finn*, the second about Rodrigo Fresán's novel *Mantra*, part of which is arranged "like a dictionary of Mexico City or a dictionary of the abyss." In his acceptance speech for the Rómulo Gallegos Prize in 1999 (Bolaño would die of liver failure four years later), he said, "So what is top-notch writing? The same thing it's always been: the ability to peer into the darkness, to leap into the void, to know that literature is basically a dangerous undertaking. The ability to sprint along the edge of the precipice: to one side the bottomless abyss and to the other the faces you love, the smiling faces you love, and books and friends and food. And the ability to accept what you find, even though it may be heavier than the stones over the graves of all dead writers. Literature, as an Andalusian folk singer would put it, is danger." The facets and designs of this danger, its depths and madness and aesthetic ends, is what Bolaño's books gravitate toward. He is like a surgeon searching for a warm heart in a corpse that can be transplanted into the open chest of a reader. The apocalyptic in his books is the apocalypse of our times (the one we're in or the one ahead we're causing) but paradoxically, or not, it's an apocalypse where there are survivors. What saves them isn't a spaceship or a bomb shelter, but a pathetic dinghy called literature floating on the seas of existence — they even emerge from the abyss smiling, the abyss that expands as *Distant Star* is an expansion of the last chapter of his *Nazi Literature in the Americas*. "After all," Bolaño writes, "literature doesn't exist anymore, only the example of it." And one hears floating up within the fathomless rift an echo of laughter...

Dear Editor,

O Julian, Julian, Julian — you had me at muffin. I am going straight out and purchasing your latest collection after I stop typing this love letter. If the poems contained within are half as entertaining as "The Gargantuan Muffin Beauty Contest" [by Julian Stannard, January 2013] I am going to be one satisfied reader. Kudos to the editors of *Poetry* for realizing that poetry does not have to be *that* serious *all* the time.

So long and thanks for all the muffins.

TINA SCHUMANN
SEATTLE, WASHINGTON

Dear Editor,

Do we find the poetry that we need or do the poems find us? Why does one open the January 2013 issue of *Poetry* to Matthew Nienow's "Ode to the Steam Box" and say, "Oh, yes. I've just seen a steam box. I want to read this. This is a poem about something in my life. How marvelous!"

I read the poem on the day after my family and I visited the site on San Diego Bay where a replica of Juan Cabrillo's *San Salvador* is being constructed. A large steam box on site allows the shipwrights to form the woods that are used for the new *San Salvador*.

Blessings on the poets who draw from these tender moments of our everyday lives.

REGINA MORIN
SAN DIEGO, CALIFORNIA

Dear Editor,

I was happy when I discovered the "Antagonisms" section in your first issue of the new year [January 2013], for when I read the game plan, I was sure we were getting a raucous meeting of the Scriblerus Club, replete with raillery and mordant wit directed at icons from the poetic canon. And the first essay, by Michael Robbins, satisfied my expectations and then some. "The Child That Sucketh Long" is reminiscent of John Dryden's sally against a poet of his day: "To some faint meaning [others] make pretense,/But Shadwell never deviates into sense."

Unfortunately, none of the other poets make much use of satire. They seem shy about letting fly. Jason Guriel gives it a go in his send-up of E.E. Cummings, but he constantly hoists himself up on a pedestal as if he's above all this childish nonsense: "Cummings seemed to have been invented to convert that stubborn student the syllabus has failed to win over to verse — or, at least, to reacquaint the kid with his inner child, the id whose appetite for nonsense and nursery rhymes has been socialized away."

I suppose. But does Guriel mean something like this?

> O what's the weather in a Beard?
> It's windy there, and rather weird,
> And when you think the sky has cleared
> — Why, there is Dirty Dinky.

That's not by Mother Goose but by Theodore Roethke, by consensus one of the important American poets of the mid-twentieth century. His appetite had not been socialized away.

WILLIAM ZANDER
NEWTON, NEW JERSEY

Dear Editor,

I enjoyed the "Antagonisms" very much. They were some of the liveliest bits of writing you have published in recent memory. Still, while I'm all for having my sacred cows butchered from time to time, I feel Mr. Cummings got it particularly bad, mostly by the dismissive hand of Michael Robbins, who writes, "Of course Thomas is a better poet than Cummings (who isn't?)."

If Mr. Robbins wants an answer to that question, he need only look in the mirror.

VINCENT FRANCONE
CHICAGO, ILLINOIS

Dear Editor,

I was so impressed by your "Antagonisms" section that it did just the opposite for me: it actually helped me appreciate my love for a few poets by knocking them off their pedestals. Too often we fail to see how good a poet really is because she is wrapped in some sort of academic gauze to preserve her (or perhaps her critics') reputation.

Thanks for a great section. While we learn much from true friends, we learn even more from dedicated antagonists. I hope you run this feature more often than every ten years.

PHIL WARD
MONTROSE, COLORADO

Dear Editor,

I can't help suspecting that you published Philip Metres's letter [January 2013] accusing Clive James of thinking that "poems exist only for the page" not only because you enjoyed the way Metres champions memorization, but also because you hoped to get many letters defending James from that accusation. Certainly I can't resist getting in on the fun.

I admire James precisely because he so obviously loves bringing alive the words of a good poem in his body. "That it can be got by heart is one of the ways we tend to define a poem," he says ["A Stretch of Verse," November 2012]. And later: "Ungaretti said that the touchstone of poetry was the hammered phrase within the singable scheme."

I was just told yesterday, *again*, that poems are really puzzles that you have to decipher. But as soon as James asks himself what a line by Auden means ("The earth turns over, our side feels the cold"), he dismisses the question: "Better for the reader to just enjoy the feeling of disorientation — or rather, of being oriented toward everywhere, a sliding universality." And if that way of putting it doesn't send you back to the poem ...

SILVINE MARBURY FARNELL
BOULDER, COLORADO

Dear Editor,

I await Lucie Brock-Broido's forthcoming book, *Stay, Illusion.* Echoes, perhaps, of Vladimir Nabokov's memoir, *Speak, Memory?*

How realistic is that thirteenth-century monk lucubrating in his dark anchorage! ["Extreme Wisteria," December 2012] At least that's how I read it while lucubrating.

Brock-Broido says she's "wildly capable of certain linguistic fabrications." Might a future one be, for instance, "The Running of the Nudes," including (take heart!) Heathcliff, Ambrose B, along with Oscar and probably even Brodsky, who has, she assures us, a "beautiful assertion." She did state her work can be "quirky."

Thank you *Poetry* for the Christmas lollipop and Brock-Broido for the fun and exhilarating answers to the questions.

BILL DUCKITT
VICTORIA, BRITISH COLUMBIA

Letters should be sent with the writer's name, address, and phone number via e-mail to editors@poetrymagazine.org. Letters may be edited for length and clarity. We regret that we cannot reply to every letter.

CONTRIBUTORS

RAE ARMANTROUT's new book is *Just Saying* (Wesleyan University Press, 2013).

DAVID BARBER's most recent collection is *Wonder Cabinet* (Northwestern University Press, 2006). He is poetry editor of the *Atlantic*.

REGINALD DWAYNE BETTS is the author of the memoir *A Question of Freedom* (Avery, 2009) and the collection of poetry *Shahid Reads His Own Palm* (Alice James Books, 2010).

DAN BROWN's most recent book of poems is *Taking the Occasion* (Ivan R. Dee, 2008), which won The New Criterion Poetry Prize. His *Why Bach?* is an online appreciation of the composer.

SHEILA P. DONOHUE* is a recipient of an Academy of American Poets prize. Her work has appeared in the *Threepenny Review*, *Prairie Schooner*, the *New England Review*, *TriQuarterly*, and *Epoch*.

JOANNE DOMINIQUE DWYER's* first book of poems, *Belle Laide*, will be published by Sarabande Books this spring. She lives in Northern New Mexico where she works with the Alzheimer's Poetry Project.

JILL ALEXANDER ESSBAUM is the author of several books of poetry including, most recently, the single-poem chapbook *The Devastation* (Cooper Dillon, 2009).

AMY GERSTLER's* most recent books are *Ghost Girl* (2004) and *Dearest Creature* (2009), both published by Penguin Books.

JASON GURIEL's next book, *The Pigheaded Soul: Essays and Reviews on Poetry and Culture* (Porcupine's Quill), will be published later this year. He lives in Toronto.

DANIEL HALPERN is the author of nine collections of poetry, most recently *Something Shining* (Alfred A. Knopf, 1999).

MICHAEL HOFMANN's next translation is Joseph Roth's last novel, *The Emperor's Tomb*, due from New Directions in April. His translations of Gottfried Benn, *Impromptus*, is due out in November from Farrar, Straus and Giroux.

DOUGLAS KEARNEY's* newest book, *Patter*, will be published by Red Hen Press in 2014. He is currently working on an opera called *Dead Horses*.

JAMES LASDUN's most recent book is a memoir, *Give Me Everything You Have: On Being Stalked* (Farrar, Straus and Giroux, 2013).

MARK LEVINE is the author of three books of poems and a nonfiction book. He teaches at the Iowa Writers' Workshop.

AMIT MAJMUDAR's most recent novel is *The Abundance* (Metropolitan Books, 2013). His most recent volume of poetry is *Heaven and Earth* (Story Line Press, 2011).

JOSHUA MEHIGAN's second book, *Accepting the Disaster*, is forthcoming from Farrar, Straus and Giroux.

ANTHONY OPAL* is an MFA candidate at Northwestern University and editor of the *Economy*. His work has appeared or is forthcoming in *Boston Review*, *TriQuarterly*, and elsewhere.

VANESSA PLACE was the first poet to perform as part of the Whitney Biennial; a content advisory was posted.

BRUCE SNIDER* is the author of two poetry collections, *Paradise, Indiana* (Louisiana State University Press, 2012) and *The Year We Studied Women* (University of Wisconsin Press, 2003).

DIANA SUDYKA is an illustrator and printmaker living and working in the Chicago area.

RACHEL JAMISON WEBSTER is the author of *September* (Northwestern University Press, 2013). She is the editor of the online anthology of international poetry, universeofpoetry.org.

JEFFREY YANG* is the author of *An Aquarium* (2008) and *Vanishing-Line* (2011), and the translator of Liu Xiaobo's *June Fourth Elegies* (2012), all published by Graywolf Press. He is also the editor of the anthology *Time of Grief: Mourning Poems* (New Directions, 2013).

* First appearance in *Poetry*.

The Robinson Jeffers Tor House 2013 Prize for Poetry

$1,000 for an original, unpublished poem not to exceed three pages. $200 for Honorable Mention

*Final Judge
Kim Addonizio*

Open to poetry in all styles, ranging from experimental to traditional forms, including short narrative poems. Each poem should be typed on 8 1/2" by 11" paper, no longer than three pages. On a cover sheet only, include name, address, telephone number, email, titles of poems; bio optional. Multiple and simultaneous submissions welcome. There is a reading fee of $10 for the first three poems; $15 for up to six poems; and $2.50 for each additional poem. Make checks or money orders payable to Tor House Foundation.
The Prize winner will be announced by May 15. Include an SASE for announcement of the Prize winner. Poems will not be returned. For more information, visit our web site or contact us by email.

The Prize for Poetry is a living memorial to American poet Robinson Jeffers (1887-1962)

Postmark Deadline for submissions is March 15, 2013. Mail poems, check or money order, and SASE to:

**Coordinator
2013 Poetry Prize
Tor House Foundation
Box 223240
Carmel, CA 93922**

Phone: 831-624-1813
Fax: 831-624-3696
www.torhouse.org
Email: thf@torhouse.org

Print of Jeffers by Barbara Whipple

The Foundation is a sponsor of National Poetry Month

Wake Forest University Press

LOUIS MACNEICE: COLLECTED POEMS

EDITED, WITH A NEW INTRODUCTION, BY PETER MACDONALD

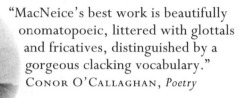

"MacNeice's best work is beautifully onomatopoeic, littered with glottals and fricatives, distinguished by a gorgeous clacking vocabulary."
CONOR O'CALLAGHAN, *Poetry*

"...one of the most arresting and accessible of modern poets".
—ANTHONY THWAITE, *The Guardian*

PAPERBACK, APPROXIMATELY 880 PAGES $23.95

CIARAN CARSON: IN THE LIGHT OF

(AFTER *Illuminations* BY ARTHUR RIMBAUD)

Ciaran Carson's version in rhyming couplets of Rimbaud's *Illuminations* proves once again what a master and magician Carson is.

"I wanted the dreamlike imagery to rhyme, chime, and echo: to make some kind of music to my ear."
—CIARAN CARSON, IN A RECENT INTERVIEW

PAPERBACK, 64 PAGES $14.95

A Volume in Celebration of *Poetry*'s Centennial

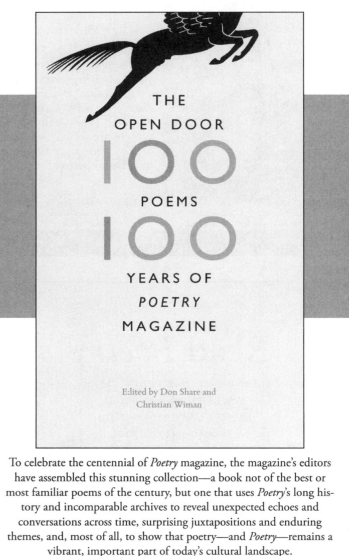

THE
OPEN DOOR

100

POEMS

100

YEARS OF
POETRY
MAGAZINE

Edited by Don Share and
Christian Wiman

To celebrate the centennial of *Poetry* magazine, the magazine's editors have assembled this stunning collection—a book not of the best or most familiar poems of the century, but one that uses *Poetry*'s long history and incomparable archives to reveal unexpected echoes and conversations across time, surprising juxtapositions and enduring themes, and, most of all, to show that poetry—and *Poetry*—remains a vibrant, important part of today's cultural landscape.

CLOTH $20.00

The University of Chicago Press • www.press.uchicago.edu

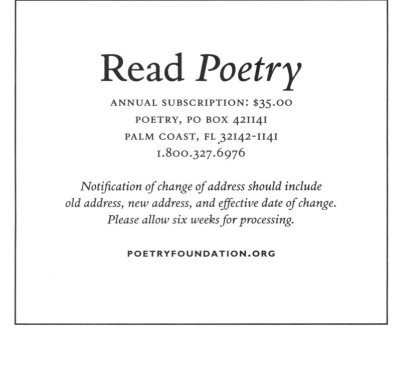